japanese

japanese

keiko ishida

Editor: Lydia Leong
Designer: Rachel Chen
Series Designer: Bernard Go Kwang Meng

This book contains previously published material from Feast of Flavours from the Japanese Kitchen

Reprinted 2009

Published by Marshall Cavendish Cuisine
An imprint of Marshall Cavendish International
1 New Industrial Road, Singapore 536196

Other Marshall Cavendish Offices:
Marshall Cavendish Ltd. 5th Floor, 32-38 Saffron Hill, London EC1N 8FH, UK • Marshall Cavendish Corporation. 99 White Plains Road, Tarrytown NY 10591-9001, USA • Marshall Cavendish International (Thailand) Co Ltd. 253 Asoke, 12th Flr, Sukhumvit 21 Road, Klongtoey Nua, Wattana, Bangkok 10110, Thailand • Marshall Cavendish (Malaysia) Sdn Bhd, Times Subang, Lot 46, Subang Hi-Tech Industrial Park, Batu Tiga, 40000 Shah Alam, Selangor Darul Ehsan, Malaysia

National Library Board Singapore Cataloguing in Publication Data

Ishida, Keiko, 1965-
Japanese / Keiko Ishida. – Singapore : Marshall Cavendish Cuisine, c2008.
p. cm. – (Mini cookbooks)
ISBN-13 : 978-981-261-568-8
ISBN-10 : 981-261-568-7

1. Cookery, Japanese. I. Title. II. Series: Mini cookbooks

TX724.5.J3
641.5952 -- dc22 OCN188431991

Printed in Singapore by Saik Wah Press Pte Ltd

contents

japanese

bean curd and seaweed miso soup Serves 4

Served at most meals, steamed rice and miso soup are the traditional staples of Japanese cuisine. For an interesting variation to this recipe, substitute the dried seaweed with vegetables such as ladies fingers, mushrooms, snow peas or chives, or use deep-fried bean curd, potatoes, bamboo shoots or white radish to replace regular bean curd.

INGREDIENTS

Soft or firm bean curd	200 g (7 oz), cut into small cubes
Dried cut seaweed (wakame)	1 Tbsp
Miso	60 g (2 oz)
Japanese spring onion (scallion)	1/4, finely sliced

DASHI

Water	800 ml (26 fl oz / 3 1/4 cups)
Dried kelp (konbu)	10-cm (4-in) piece
Bonito flakes	25 g (1 oz)

NOTE

To save time when cooking, make an instant stock by dissolving 1 1/3 tsp dashi powder in 700 ml (22 fl oz / 2 3/4 cups) water.

METHOD

- Prepare dashi. Put water and kelp into a saucepan and leave for 30 minutes. Place over medium heat and when small bubbles appear from the bottom, remove kelp.
- When water is boiling, add bonito flakes, then reduce heat and simmer for a few seconds. Remove from heat, then leave until bonito flakes sink to the bottom of saucepan. Strain stock and discard solids.
- Return strained stock to the saucepan and add bean curd and seaweed. Bring to the boil, then remove from heat. Strain miso into soup, then stir until miso has dissolved.
- Reheat soup and return to the boil, then remove from heat immediately. Garnish with sliced spring onion and serve hot.

miso soup with pork and vegetables Serves 4

Substantial enough to be served as a main dish, this speciality originates from northern Japan, and is traditionally served at festivities held by the riverside during autumn.

INGREDIENTS

Sesame oil	2 Tbsp
Pork belly or pork shoulder	150 g (5 1/3 oz), thinly sliced into bite-size pieces
Potatoes	2, small, peeled, cut into cubes, then soaked and drained just before use
Carrot	1/2, peeled, thinly sliced into rounds, then quartered
White radish (daikon)	6-cm (2 1/2-in) length, peeled, thinly sliced into rounds, then quartered
Konnyaku packed in water	130 g (4 1/2 oz), drained and cut into thick matchsticks, then blanched and drained
Burdock (gobo)	70 g (2 1/2 oz), scrubbed clean and cut into small pieces
Shiitake mushrooms	2, stems discarded and thinly sliced
Deep-fried bean curd (abura age)	1, cut into thin strips
Sake	2 Tbsp
Miso	60–70 g (2–2 1/2 oz)
Japanese spring onion (scallion)	1, finely sliced

DASHI

Water	1 litre (32 fl oz / 4 cups)
Dried kelp (konbu)	12-cm (5-in) piece
Bonito flakes	30 g (1 oz)

GARNISH

Japanese spring onion (scallion)
Shichimi togarashi (optional)

METHOD

- Prepare dashi. Refer to method on page 10.
- Heat sesame oil in a saucepan and stir-fry pork, potatoes, carrot, radish, konnyaku and burdock over medium heat for 2–3 minutes.
- Add dashi and simmer for about 10 minutes, then add mushrooms and bean curd. Simmer for 2–3 minutes, skimming off any foam that rises to the surface.
- Turn off heat, add sake and strain miso into soup. Stir until miso has dissolved. Add spring onion and reheat. When soup is almost boiling, remove from heat.
- Ladle soup into individual serving bowls. Garnish with sliced spring onion and sprinkle with shichimi togarashi, if desired. Serve hot.

tokyo-style new year's soup Serves 4

While rice cake soup is traditionally served on 1st January to celebrate the New Year in Japan, the recipe for the soup differs from region to region. This recipe hails from Tokyo, hence, its name.

INGREDIENTS

Chicken thighs	120 g (4½ oz), skinned, fat removed and deboned, then cut into small pieces
Sake	1 tsp
White radish (daikon)	6-cm (2½-in) length, peeled, thinly sliced into rounds, then quartered
Carrot	¼ peeled and cut into shapes with a vegetable cutter
Fresh shiitake mushrooms	2, stems discarded, shallow cuts made on caps to form desired pattern
Pink-swirled fish paste cake (naruto)	8 slices, each about 0.5-cm (¼-in) thick
Rice cakes	4, each about 50 g (2 oz)

DASHI

Water	1 litre (32 fl oz / 4 cups)
Dried kelp (konbu)	12-cm (5-in) piece
Bonito flakes	30 g (1 oz)

SEASONING

Sake	1 Tbsp
Salt	½–⅔ tsp
Light soy sauce	¼ tsp

GARNISH

Trefoil (mitsuba)	1 small bunch, cut into 2-cm (¾-in) lengths
Yuzu rind	1 small piece, cut into fine strips

METHOD

- Prepare dashi. Refer to method on page 10.
- Marinate chicken with sake and leave for about 10 minutes.
- Pour dashi into a medium-size pot and bring to the boil. Add chicken, radish, carrot, mushrooms and fish paste cake. Cook for about 10 minutes.
- While soup is boiling, grill rice cakes in a preheated oven at 200°C (400°F) or toaster for 5–10 minutes, until slightly puffy and light brown in colour.
- Mix seasoning ingredients together and stir into soup. Remove from heat.
- Place a grilled or toasted rice cake into each individual serving bowl and ladle soup over. Garnish with trefoil and yuzu rind. Serve hot.

short-neck clam clear soup Serves 4

Enjoy this clear soup with a rich-tasting stock, sweetened by the natural juices of the clams. You can also add seaweed, mushrooms and fish paste to the soup for a more substantial dish. If short-neck clams are unavailable, substitute with any other kind of clams.

INGREDIENTS

Salt	1/4 tsp
Short-neck clams	300 g (11 oz)
Sake	1 Tbsp
Light soy sauce	1 Tbsp
Myoga ginger flower buds	2, thinly sliced

STOCK

Water	700 ml (22 fl oz / 2 3/4 cups)
Dried kelp (konbu)	10-cm (4-in) piece

METHOD

- Dissolve 1 tsp salt in a basin of water and soak clams for about 30 minutes to remove any grit. Rinse well, then drain and set aside.
- Prepare stock. Put water and kelp into a medium saucepan and leave for 30 minutes. Cook over medium heat and when small bubbles appear from the bottom, remove kelp.
- Reheat stock and when it comes to the boil, add clams. Return to the boil, then reduce heat and skim off any foam that rises to the surface.
- Season stock with remaining salt, sake and light soy sauce. Simmer for 3 minutes, or until clams open. Discard any clams that remain closed.
- Ladle into individual serving bowls and garnish with sliced ginger flower buds. Serve hot.

cucumber and octopus salad with sweet vinegar dressing

Serves 4

This is a refreshing and light salad with a non-oily dressing.

INGREDIENTS

Japanese cucumbers	2
Salt	1 tsp
Boiled octopus tentacle	150 g (5 1/3 oz), roll-cut into 2.5-cm (1-in) wedges
Old ginger	3-cm (1 1/4-in) knob, peeled and finely shredded, then soaked in ice water and drained before use

SWEET VINEGAR DRESSING

Rice vinegar	3 Tbsp
Sugar	3 Tbsp
Salt	1 tsp
Light soy sauce	1/2 tsp

METHOD

- Prepare sweet vinegar dressing. Put all ingredients into a small bowl and mix, using fingers, until completely dissolved. Set aside.
- Rub cucumbers with salt to smoothen skins, then rinse and roll-cut into wedges.
- Chill ingredients and dressing separately in the fridge until ready to serve.
- To serve, combine chilled cucumbers and octopus in a salad bowl. Drizzle with sweet vinegar dressing and toss to mix well. Spoon onto individual plates and top with shredded ginger. Serve immediately.

deep-fried bean curd Serves 4

Bean curd is a very popular ingredient in Japanese cooking. It is rich in protein and low in calories.

INGREDIENTS

Soft or firm bean curd	2 slabs, total 600 g (1 lb 5$^{1}/_{3}$ oz), cut into large pieces and pat dry
Egg	1, lightly beaten
Potato flour (potato starch) for coating	
Cooking oil for deep-frying	
Green shishito chillies	12, washed, pat dry and pierced
Light soy sauce	1 Tbsp
Mirin	1 tsp

DASHI

Water	150 ml (5 fl oz)
Dried kelp (konbu)	5-cm (2-in) piece
Bonito flakes	10 g ($^{1}/_{3}$ oz)

GARNISH

Finely sliced Japanese spring onion (scallion)	to taste
Grated old ginger	to taste
Fine dried bonito flakes	to taste

METHOD

- Prepare dashi. Refer to method on page 10.
- Dip bean curd into beaten egg and coat with potato flour. Heat oil to 170°C (350°F) and deep-fry bean curd until golden. Remove and drain on kitchen paper.
- Scald shishito chillies in hot oil to preserve colour. Remove immediately and drain on kitchen paper.
- Prepare sauce. Heat 100 ml (3½ fl oz)dashi, light soy sauce and mirin in a small saucepan and bring to the boil. Remove from heat.
- Arrange deep-dried bean curd and shishito chillies in individual serving dishes and pour sauce over. Serve hot, garnished with spring onions, grated ginger and fine dried bonito flakes to taste.

と
ノアキ
ント
エブ
拡な
にする

simmered hijiki seaweed Serves 4

Hijiki seaweed contains a lot of calcium and is available dried, all year round. This popular side dish goes well with steamed rice.

INGREDIENTS

Dark soy sauce	4 Tbsp
Sugar	3 Tbsp
Mirin	2 Tbsp
Dried hiijiki seaweed	35–40 g (1–1 1/2 oz), soaked for 20 minutes and drained
Carrot	80 g (3 oz), peeled and shredded
Deep-fried bean curd (abura age)	2, blanched and cut into long strips

DASHI

Water	250 ml (8 fl oz / 1 cup)
Dried kelp (konbu)	5-cm (2-in) piece
Bonito flakes	10 g (1/3 oz)

GARNISH

Ground toasted white sesame seeds	to taste

METHOD

- Prepare dashi. Refer to method on page 10.
- Pour dashi, soy sauce, sugar and mirin into a medium saucepan. Bring to the boil and add seaweed, carrot and deep-fried bean curd. Lower heat and simmer for 10–15 minutes, stirring occasionally, until most of the liquid is absorbed.
- Garnish with ground toasted sesame seeds and serve immediately, or chill before serving, if desired.

savoury egg custard (chawan mushi) Serves 4

In Japan, this dish is prepared in traditional chawan mushi cups with lids. If you do not have these cups, use porcelain rice bowls or ramekins as substitutes.

INGREDIENTS

Chicken thighs	50 g (2 oz), skinned and deboned, fat removed and cubed
Sake	1 tsp
Salt	a pinch
Eggs	3, lightly beaten
Salt	1 tsp
Light soy sauce	1 tsp
Prawns (shrimps)	8, large, peeled and deveined
Gingko nuts	8, shelled
Fresh shiitake mushrooms	2, stems discarded and finely sliced
Pink-swirled fish paste cake (naruto) or fish paste of choice	4 slices, each 0.5-cm (1/4-in) thick
Trefoil (mitsuba)	4 stalks, finely sliced

DASHI

Water	600 ml (20 fl oz / 2 1/2 cups)
Dried kelp (konbu)	8-cm (3 1/4-in) piece
Bonito flakes	20 g (2/3 oz)

GARNISH

Flower-shaped flour pieces

METHOD

- Prepare dashi. Measure out 500 ml (16 fl oz / 2 cups). Refer to method on page 10.
- Marinate chicken with sake and salt for 10 minutes.
- Lightly mix together eggs, salt, soy sauce and dashi. Strain using a fine sieve.
- Divide chicken, prawns, gingko nuts, mushrooms and fish paste cake equally among 4 steaming cups or bowls. Gently pour an equal amount of egg mixture into each cup or bowl, then top with 1 flower-shaped flour piece. Cover with lids or aluminium foil if lids are unavailable, to ensure custard has a smooth surface when steamed.
- Place in a steamer and steam over high heat for 1 minute, then reduce heat to low and steam for about 12 minutes until egg mixture is set. Remove from heat and serve hot.

vegetables with bean curd dressing Serves 4

This dish is part of the vegetarian diet observed in Japanese Buddhist temples.

INGREDIENTS

Spinach	70 g (2½ oz), roots discarded and washed
Sake	1 Tbsp
Light soy sauce	1 Tbsp
Carrot	1, small, peeled and julienned
Dried shiitake mushrooms	4, soaked in warm water for 1 hour, stems discarded and finely sliced

DASHI

Water	250 ml (8 fl oz / 1 cup)
Dried kelp (konbu)	5-cm (2-in) piece
Bonito flakes	10 g (⅓ oz)

BEAN CURD DRESSING

Soft or firm bean curd	300 g (11 oz), cut into small pieces and blanched
Sugar	2 Tbsp
Light soy sauce	2 tsp
Salt	⅓ tsp
White sesame paste	5 Tbsp
Mirin	1 Tbsp

METHOD

- Prepare dashi. Refer to method on page 10.
- Blanch spinach in salted boiling water for a few seconds, then rinse under tap water. Drain well and cut into 4-cm ($1^{3}/_{4}$-in) lengths. Set aside.
- Pour 200 ml ($6^{1}/_{2}$ fl oz)dashi, sake and light soy sauce into a medium saucepan. Bring to the boil, add carrot and mushrooms, then lower heat and simmer for 5–10 minutes until most of the liquid is absorbed. Drain simmered vegetables well. Set aside.
- Prepare bean curd dressing. Wrap bean curd in a clean piece of muslin or cotton cloth and squeeze gently to remove as much liquid as possible. Mash bean curd in a grinding bowl, then add remaining ingredients for dressing. Mix well and place in a salad bowl.
- Add spinach and simmered vegetables to bean curd dressing. Toss well and serve immediately.

french beans with sesame dressing Serves 4

This is a popular home-style side dish that is both delicious and easy to make. If French beans are unavailable, substitute with other vegetables such as spinach, carrots, burdock, lotus root, broccoli or aubergine (eggplant/brinjal).

INGREDIENTS

French beans	200g (7 oz), washed and trimmed
Black or white sesame seeds	6 Tbsp
Dark soy sauce	2 Tbsp
Sugar	3 Tbsp

METHOD

- Blanch French beans in a pot of salted boiling water for 2–3 minutes. Drain in a flat sieve, then dry and cool by fanning vegetables with a hand-held fan, or plunge into ice water, then drain and pat dry.
- Cut French beans into 4-cm (1 ¾-in) lengths and set aside.
- Toast sesame seeds in a medium pan over low heat until aromatic. Transfer to a grinding bowl (suri bachi) and grind until fine. Add soy sauce and sugar. Mix well.
- Transfer French beans to a large bowl. Toss well with ground sesame mixture. Dish out and serve immediately.

simmered chinese flowering cabbage and deep-fried bean curd Serves 4

This dish uses a cooking method known as nibitashi that involves simmering vegetables in soup.

INGREDIENTS

Chinese flowering cabbage	300 g (11 oz), roots discarded
Deep-fried bean curd (abura age)	2
Sugar	2 tsp
Sake	2 Tbsp
Light soy sauce	2½ Tbsp
Toasted white sesame seeds	to taste (optional)

DASHI

Water	500 ml (16 fl oz / 2 cups)
Dried kelp (konbu)	10-cm (4-in) piece
Bonito flakes	20 g (⅔ oz)

METHOD

- Prepare dashi. Refer to method on page 10.
- Wash Chinese flowering cabbage and drain well. Cut into 4-cm (1¾-in) lengths, separating leaves and stalks.
- Blanch deep-fried bean curd with boiling water to remove any smell and oil. Drain and halve each bean curd lengthways, then cut across into long strips.
- Add dashi, sugar, sake and light soy sauce to a medium saucepan. Bring to the boil, then add bean curd strips and vegetable stalks. Lower heat and simmer for 1–2 minutes until stalks are almost cooked. Add leaves and simmer for another 1–2 minutes. Remove from heat.
- Ladle soup into individual bowls and sprinkle sesame seeds over, if desired. Serve hot.

simmered lotus root Serves 4

Known in Japan as renkon no kimpira, this dish is named after a popular character in Joruri, a traditional Japanese play set during the Edo period. Kimpira was renowned for his superhuman strength, and it is believed that eating this healthy dish will keep one strong like Kimpira. If lotus root is unavailable, substitute with burdock, carrots, potatoes or white radish.

INGREDIENTS

Lotus root	200g (7 oz), washed and peeled
Dried red chilli	1, finely cut with a pair of scissors
Sesame oil	1 Tbsp
Toasted white sesame seeds	1 Tbsp

SEASONING

Dark soy sauce	1 1/2 Tbsp
Sugar	1 Tbsp
Sake	1 Tbsp
Mirin	1 Tbsp

METHOD

- Roll cut lotus root into wedges, then soak in water. Drain when ready to use.
- Bring a pot of water to the boil, then add drained lotus root and boil for about 5 minutes. Drain and set aside.
- Combine seasoning ingredients in a small bowl. Blend well until sugar has dissolved. Set aside.
- Heat sesame oil in a frying pan over medium heat, then add chilli and lotus root. Stir-fry for 1 minute. Add seasoning, then stir to mix well. Simmer for 1–2 minutes until most of the liquid is absorbed and lotus root is well-coated with a glossy sauce.
- Remove from heat and dish out. Garnish with sesame seeds before serving.

pan-fried aubergines with miso sauce Serves 4

When I was a child, my mother often prepared this dish for the family. A quick and simple recipe, it remains one of my favourite dishes today.

INGREDIENTS

Cooking oil	3 Tbsp
Sesame oil	3 Tbsp
Japanese aubergines (eggplants/ brinjals)	6, washed, ends trimmed and cut into 1-cm (1/2-in) thick rounds
Toasted white sesame seeds	to taste (optional)

SEASONING

Miso	3 Tbsp
Sugar	3 Tbsp
Mirin	2 Tbsp
Sake	3 Tbsp
Water	2 Tbsp

METHOD

- Combine seasoning ingredients in a small bowl and mix well. Set aside.
- Heat both types of oil in a frying pan. Add aubergines and pan-fry for 3–5 minutes on both sides until brown.
- Pour seasoning mixture over aubergine slices, stirring gently to mix well. Simmer over low heat for 2–3 minutes until sauce has thickened and aubergines are well-coated.
- Remove from heat and dish out. Garnish with sesame seeds, if desired, before serving.

simmered pumpkin Serves 4

Pumpkin is a summer vegetable with lots of vitamins. When buying pumpkins, choose those with bright orange-coloured flesh as they are sweeter. The vegetable is cooked simply in this recipe, creating a very refreshing dish.

INGREDIENTS

Japanese pumpkin	600 g (1 lb $5^{1}/_{3}$ oz), seeded, washed and left with skin on
Water	200 ml ($6^{1}/_{2}$ fl oz)
Sugar	2 Tbsp
Mirin	1 Tbsp
Light soy sauce	1 tsp
Salt	a pinch
Toasted white sesame seeds	to taste

METHOD

- Cut pumpkin into 5 × 6-cm (2 × $2^{1}/_{2}$-in) pieces. Bevel the edges of each piece on the skin side.
- Put pumpkin, water and sugar in a medium saucepan, then cover with a drop-in lid, or a sheet of baking paper trimmed to fit pan. Simmer over medium heat for 2–3 minutes.
- Add mirin, soy sauce and salt. Reduce heat to low and simmer for 5–10 minutes, or until pumpkin has softened.
- Remove from heat and dish out. Garnish with sesame seeds and serve.

simmered radish with minced chicken Serves 4

Radish is great for simmering in dishes with meat or poultry, as it can absorb the flavours of the other ingredients fully during the slow-cooking process. Turnips and pumpkins are also good substitutes for radish in this recipe.

INGREDIENTS

White radish (daikon)	600 g (1lb $5\frac{1}{3}$ oz), peeled and cut into 2.5-cm (1-in) thick rounds
Raw rice grains (any kind except Basmati or fragrant Thai)	1 Tbsp
Salt	$\frac{1}{2}$ tsp
Light soy sauce	$\frac{1}{2}$ tsp
Minced chicken	150 g ($5\frac{1}{3}$ oz)
Mirin	1 Tbsp
Sugar	1 Tbsp
Dark soy sauce	1 Tbsp
Ginger juice	1 tsp
Potato flour (potato starch)	$\frac{1}{2}$ Tbsp, mixed with 1 Tbsp water
Old ginger	4-cm ($1\frac{3}{4}$-in) knob, peeled, finely shredded, then soaked and drained before use

DASHI

Water	500 ml (16 fl oz / 2 cups)
Dried kelp (konbu)	10-cm (4-in) piece
Bonito flakes	20 g ($\frac{2}{3}$ oz)

METHOD

- Prepare dashi. Refer to method on page 10.
- Bevel the edge of each round of radish on both sides. Make a cross-shape incision on one side of each round. Place radish and rice into a large pot and cover with water. Boil over medium heat for 20 minutes, until radish is cooked and just tender.
- Drain and discard rice and water, then rinse radish under tap water lightly to remove all bitter juices and rice starch. Drain.
- Add dashi, salt and soy sauce to a large pot. Bring to the boil, then add cooked radish and simmer over low heat for 5 minutes. Remove radish from stock and set aside.
- Add minced chicken, mirin, sugar, dark soy sauce and ginger juice to stock. Mix well and bring to the boil, then stir in potato flour mixture to thicken sauce. Remove from heat.
- Divide radish among individual serving bowls and ladle sauce over. Garnish with shredded ginger and serve hot.

broiled yellowtail Serves 2

The Japanese cooking method of broiling imbues any fish or meat with a fragrant soy sauce flavour. Feel free to substitute with other kinds of seafood such as Spanish mackerel, salmon and squid, if desired.

INGREDIENTS

Cooking oil	1 Tbsp
Japanese yellowtail fillets	2, each about 100 g (3 1/2 oz)
Japanese spring onion (scallion)	1/2, cut into 4-cm (1 3/4-in) lengths
Ground Japanese pepper (sansho)	to taste (optional)

SEASONING

Dark soy sauce	1 1/2 Tbsp
Mirin	1 1/2 Tbsp
Sake	1 1/2 Tbsp

METHOD

- Combine seasoning ingredients and set aside.
- Heat cooking oil in a medium frying pan. Pan-fry yellowtail fillets and spring onion over medium-high heat. When spring onion is lightly browned, remove from pan and set aside.
- Cover, if required, and continue to pan-fry fish fillets for another 1–2 minutes, or until golden brown and crisp on both sides.
- Return spring onion to pan and add seasoning. Cook for another 1–2 minutes, until sauce is reduced and fillets are well coated.
- Arrange fish on individual serving plates with spring onion. Serve, sprinkled with ground Japanese pepper, if desired.

grilled mackerel with white miso paste Serves 2

A local dish in Kyoto, the main seasoning ingredient used is white miso or saikyo miso, a local speciality of the prefecture. The taste of this soy bean paste is sweeter than other varieties, and goes well with many kinds of seafood. Substitute Spanish mackerel with yellowtail, sea bream, salmon, squid, scallop or white promfret, if preferred.

INGREDIENTS

Spanish mackerel fillets	2, each about 100 g (3½ oz)
Salt	¼ tsp

PICKLED LOTUS ROOT

Rice vinegar	5 Tbsp
Water	500 ml (16 fl oz / 2 cups)
Lotus root	200 g (7 oz)
Sugar	1½ Tbsp
Salt	⅓ tsp

MARINADE

White miso	100 g (3½ oz)
Brown miso	30 g (1 oz)
Mirin	1 Tbsp
Sake	1 Tbsp
Sugar	1 Tbsp

NOTE

Other hardy root vegetables like white radish, carrot and turnip can also be used for pickling in place of lotus root.

METHOD

- Prepare this dish at least 1 day ahead.
- Prepare pickled lotus root. Stir 1 Tbsp rice vinegar into water. Set aside. Wash and peel lotus root, then slice into 0.3-cm (1/10-in) rounds. Trim into flower shapes if desired. Soak in vinegar solution immediately for about 5 minutes to prevent discolouration. Drain and blanch in boiling water for 1–2 minutes until tender, but still crisp. Remove and drain well. Stir sugar and salt into 4 Tbsp rice vinegar until completely dissolved. Transfer mixture to a clean plastic bag and add lotus root. Seal and shake well. Refrigerate for at least 1 hour before use. Pickled lotus root can be kept refrigerated for up to 3 days,

- Sprinkle fish fillets with salt and refrigerate for 30 minutes. Combine ingredients for marinade and set aside. Remove fish from refrigerator and pat dry with kitchen paper. Wrap fish in a clean piece of cotton gauze or muslin cloth. Put half the amount of marinade in a plastic container and add wrapped fish. Pour remaining marinade over. Cover and refrigerate overnight, or for up to 1 week.
- To cook, unwrap fish and pat dry with kitchen paper. Grill over medium heat for 2–3 minutes on one side, then turn fish over and grill other side for another 2–3 minutes until brown.
- Alternatively, grill fish fillets in a preheated oven at 200°C (400°F), skin side up, for 10 minutes. Turn fish over and grill other side for 5 minutes, or until brown.
- Arrange fish on individual serving plates. Serve hot with pickled lotus root on the side.

simmered mackerel in grated radish Serves 4

This dish is known as saba no mizore ni In Japanese, which means "mackerel simmered with sleet", as the grated radish resembles sleet.

INGREDIENTS

Mackerel fillet	600 g (1 lb 5 1/3 oz), cleaned
Salt	1/2 tsp
Plain (all-purpose) flour	2 Tbsp
Cooking oil for deep-frying	
Sugar	1 Tbsp
Sake	3 Tbsp
Mirin	1 Tbsp
Dark soy sauce	2 Tbsp
White radish (daikon)	200 g (7 oz), peeled, grated and drained of bitter juice
Spring onions (scallions)	2, cut into 4-cm (1 3/4-in) lengths

DASHI

Water	150 ml (5 fl oz)
Dried kelp (konbu)	5-cm (2-in) piece
Bonito flakes	5 g (1/6 oz)

METHOD

- Prepare dashi. Refer to method on page 10.
- Place mackerel on a flat sieve over a large bowl and sprinkle salt all over. Leave for 10 minutes to drain. Cut fish into large pieces and pat dry with kitchen paper.
- Heat oil for deep-frying to 180°C (350°F). Coat fish with flour, shaking off any excess. Deep-fry for 3–5 minutes, or until golden and crispy. Drain on kitchen paper.
- Add dashi, sugar, sake, mirin and soy sauce to a saucepan. Bring to the boil, then add deep-fried mackerel. Reduce heat to medium and simmer for 2–3 minutes. Add grated radish and spring onions and return to the boil, then remove from heat immediately.
- Dish out to a large serving bowl and serve hot.

salt-grilled horse mackerel Serves 4

Grilling is a popular cooking method for fish in Japanese cuisine. Many kinds of fish can be grilled including Spanish mackerel, bream, Pacific saury and sardine. Sardine and Pacific saury do not have to be gutted before cooking.

INGREDIENTS

Horse mackerel	4, medium
Salt	1 Tbsp
White radish (daikon)	10-cm (4-in) length, peeled and grated
Dark soy sauce	to taste
Lemon juice	(optional)

GARNISH

Oba leaves

Lemon slices

METHOD

- Remove gills and gut fish, then rinse and pat dry with kitchen paper. Place cleaned fish on a flat sieve over a metal bowl to drain well.
- Just before grilling, sprinkle salt all over fish and coat tail and fins with salt.
- Heat a grill pan over medium heat on a gas hob until smoking, then grill fish on each side for 1–2 minutes until brown.
- Place grated radish on a cloth in a fine sieve, then rinse briefly under tap water. Squeeze lightly to drain away bitter juices.
- Arrange fish, a small mound of drained radish drizzled with soy sauce to taste, oba leaves and lemon slices on a large serving plate. Sprinkle a little lemon juice over fish just before serving, if desired.

simmered squid and taro Serves 4

In Japan, the availability of satoimo taro at the markets heralds the beginning of the autumn season for many people. If satoimo taro is unavailable, substitute with new potatoes, which are just as tasty. Frozen, ready-to-use satoimo can also be bought at many Asian supermarkets today.

INGREDIENTS

Satoimo taro	8, each about 60 g (2 oz)
Salt	1/2 tsp
Squid	1, about 300 g (11 oz), or 3–4 small squid, gutted and cleaned, then cut into 1-cm (1/2-in) thick rings
Dark soy sauce	2 Tbsp
Sugar	2 Tbsp
Sake	2 Tbsp
Old ginger	4-cm (1 3/4-in) knob, peeled and cut into 0.3-cm (1/10-in) slices
Mirin	1 Tbsp

DASHI

Water	400 ml (13 fl oz)
Dried kelp (konbu)	5-cm (2-in) piece
Bonito flakes	10 g (1/3 oz)

METHOD

- Prepare dashi. Refer to method on page 10.
- Wash and peel satoimo taro, then rub with salt and rinse under tap water to remove sticky juices. Cover taro with water in a pot, then bring to the boil. Continue boiling for another 2–3 minutes. Remove from heat, drain and set aside.
- Put soy sauce, sugar, sake, sliced ginger and dashi into a pot. Bring to the boil, then add squid and taro and simmer for 15 minutes, or until taro and squid are very tender.
- Add mirin and simmer for another 1–2 minutes, until heated through. Remove from heat.
- Transfer to a serving bowl and serve hot.

simmered red snapper Serves 4

This dish is known as tai no nitsuke in Japan, where "nitsuke" refers to the Japanese cooking technique of simmering food in sake, sugar or mirin and soy sauce. This cooking method is very popular for many kinds of fish including yellowtail, sardine, salmon and flatfish.

INGREDIENTS

Burdock (gobo)	140 g (5 oz), washed and scrubbed clean
Water	200 ml (6½ fl oz)
Sake	4 Tbsp
Sugar	3 Tbsp
Dark soy sauce	3 Tbsp
Old ginger	4-cm (1¾-in) knob, peeled and sliced
Red snapper fillets	4, each about 100 g (3½ oz)

GARNISH

Japanese spring onion (scallion)	½, white portion only, cut into 6-cm (2½-in) lengths

METHOD

- Cut burdock into 5-cm (2-in) lengths and quarter lengthways. Soak in water and set aside.
- Shred spring onion for garnish finely lengthways. Soak in ice water and set aside. Drain before use.
- Combine water, sake, sugar, soy sauce and sliced ginger in a medium frying pan and bring to the boil. When boiling, add burdock and place fish in pan, skin side up. Cover with a drop-in lid, or a sheet of baking paper trimmed to fit pan. Simmer over medium-high heat for about 10 minutes, or until fish is cooked. Remove from heat.
- Arrange simmered fish on individual serving plates. Spoon some sauce over. Serve, garnished with simmered burdock and spring onion on the side.

braised beef and potatoes Serves 4

This recipe belongs to my mother and it is one of my favourites. Ask your local butcher for thinly sliced beef of a tender cut that is suitable for a simmered sukiyaki dish. Packaged sukiyaki-style beef is also available at the chilled section of most Japanese supermarkets.

INGREDIENTS

Sesame oil	1 1/2 Tbsp
White onions	1 1/2, peeled and cut into wedges along the grain
Thinly sliced beef	200 g (7 oz), cut into bite-size pieces
Potatoes	4, medium, peeled and cut into chunks, soaked, then drained before use
Carrot	1, medium, peeled and roll-cut into wedges
Hot water	300 ml (10 fl oz / 1 1/4 cups)
French beans	90 g (3 oz), trimmed and cut into 4-cm (1 3/4-in) lengths, then blanched

SEASONING

Sugar	1 1/2 Tbsp
Mirin	1 1/2 Tbsp
Dark soy sauce	2 1/2–3 Tbsp

METHOD

- Combine seasoning ingredients in a small bowl. Mix well and set aside.
- Heat oil in a pot over high heat, then add onions and beef. Stir-fry for 1–2 minutes, then add seasoning and simmer briefly until all liquid is absorbed.
- Add potatoes, carrot and hot water. Cover and simmer over medium-high heat for about 15 minutes, or until sauce is mostly absorbed.
- Stir in French beans and simmer for 1 minute to heat through. Remove from heat.
- Transfer to a serving bowl and serve hot with rice, if desired.

japanese-style deep-fried chicken Serves 4

This crispy chicken dish is absolutely delicious. It is popular with children and adults alike.

INGREDIENTS

Boneless chicken thighs	500 g (1 lb 1½ oz)
Dark soy sauce	2 Tbsp
Sake	1 Tbsp
Mirin	1 Tbsp
Ginger juice	2 tsp
Potato flour (potato starch)	5 Tbsp
Vegetable oil for deep-frying	
Lemon wedges	

METHOD

- Pierce chicken thighs with a metal or bamboo skewer several times to enable meat to fully absorb seasoning. Cut into 4 × 5-cm (1¾ × 2-in) pieces and place in a large bowl.
- Add soy sauce, sake, mirin and ginger juice to chicken and mix well. Set aside to marinate for about 30 minutes.
- Drain marinated chicken and pat dry thoroughly with kitchen paper.
- Coat with potato flour, shaking off any excess, then deep-fry in small batches in hot oil at 170°C (340°F) for 5–7 minutes, until brown and crisp. Drain on kitchen paper.
- Transfer to a serving plate and serve hot with lemon wedges on the side.

pan-fried ginger pork Serves 4

This is one of my favourite quick-and-easy recipes. I prepare it whenever I am pressed for time.

INGREDIENTS

Pork tenderloin (fillet)	500 g (1 lb 1 1/2 oz), cut into 0.5-cm (1/4-in) thick slices
Sake	3 Tbsp
Dark soy sauce	2 Tbsp
Mirin	2 Tbsp
Sesame oil	2 tsp
Sugar	2 tsp
Grated old ginger	2 Tbsp
Grated garlic	2 tsp
Cooking oil	1 Tbsp

PARSLEY POTATOES

Potatoes	2, medium, peeled and cubed
Finely chopped parsley	1 tsp
Ground black pepper	to taste
Salt	to taste

GARNISH

White radish sprouts	a small bunch, soaked in ice water and drained before use
Cherry tomatoes	2–3, halved

METHOD

- Prepare parsley potatoes. Boil potato cubes for 10–15 minutes until soft and cooked. Drain thoroughly and place in a mixing bowl. Sprinkle with chopped parsley, pepper and salt, then toss to mix well. Set aside.
- Marinate pork in 1 Tbsp sake for 5 minutes. In a small bowl, whisk together soy sauce, mirin, 2 Tbsp sake, sesame oil, sugar, ginger and garlic until well-blended. Set aside.
- Heat oil in a frying pan over high heat. Stir-fry pork for 1–2 minutes, until meat changes colour. Add seasoning mixture to pan and simmer for 1–2 minutes until pork is cooked. Remove from heat.
- Transfer to a serving plate. Arrange potatoes on the side and garnish with radish sprouts and cherry tomatoes. Serve with rice and a simple green salad, if desired.

deep-fried breaded pork cutlets Serves 4

Although deep-fried breaded pork cutlets are commonly served at many Japanese restaurants, they are fairly simple to prepare at home.

INGREDIENTS

Pork loin cutlets	4, boneless, each about 100 g (3 1/2 oz), and 1.5-cm (3/4-in) thick
Milk	100 ml (3 1/2 fl oz)
Sake	100 ml (3 1/2 fl oz)
Black pepper	to taste
Salt	to taste
Plain (all-purpose) flour	4 Tbsp
Egg	1, large, beaten
Dried breadcrumbs	55 g (2 oz)
White sesame seeds	4 Tbsp, toasted and ground
Japanese hot mustard	to taste
Cooking oil for deep-frying	

SAUCE

Store-bought tonkatsu pork cutlet sauce	to taste
Ground toasted white sesame seeds	to taste

METHOD

- Marinate pork cutlets in milk and sake for about 10 minutes. Drain and pat dry with kitchen paper. Make a few cuts on each piece of pork between the fat and lean parts. Tenderise cutlets briefly with a meat mallet, or the spine of a cleaver. Season with pepper and salt to taste. Coat each cutlet with flour, shaking off any excess. Dip into beaten egg and coat well with breadcrumbs.

- Heat oil to 160°–170°C (325°–340°F). Deep-fry pork cutlets, 1–2 pieces at a time, for about 5 minutes until golden brown. Remove and drain on kitchen paper. Repeat until all cutlets are deep-fried.

- Cut deep-fried cutlets crossways into 1.5-cm (3/4-in) strips. Arrange on individual serving plates, accompanied by some cabbage, tomato and lemon wedges, cucumber slices and a dollop of Japanese hot mustard on the side, if desired.

- Serve hot, with individual bowls of ready-to-use tonkatsu dipping sauce, topped with ground sesame seeds.

teriyaki chicken Serves 4

Teriyaki means "broil" in Japanese. Teriyaki sauce goes extremely well with mayonnaise.

INGREDIENTS

Boneless chicken thighs	400 g (14 1/3 oz)
Cooking oil	2 Tbsp
Dark soy sauce	2 Tbsp
Mirin	2 Tbsp
Sake	2 Tbsp
Mayonnaise	to taste
Ground Japanese pepper (sansho)	to taste

GARNISH

White radish (daikon)	1/4, peeled and finely julienned
White radish sprouts	1 small bunch, cut into 3-cm (1 1/4-in) lengths, soaked in ice water and drained before use

METHOD

- Trim and discard excess fat from chicken thighs. Make a few deep cuts in the thickest part of the flesh.
- Heat oil in a frying pan over high heat. Place chicken in, skin side down. Cover pan with lid and pan-fry for about 2 minutes. Remove lid, turn chicken over and replace lid. Lower to medium heat and pan-fry other side of chicken for about 5 minutes, until brown and cooked.
- Combine soy sauce, mirin and sake in a small bowl, then pour over chicken in pan. Cook for about 1 minute, or until chicken is well-coated and sauce is reduced. Remove from heat.
- Arrange chicken on a serving plate and sprinkle ground Japanese pepper over, if desired. Garnish with shredded white radish and radish sprouts. Serve with mayonnaise on the side.

chicken and eggs on rice Serves 4

This dish is known as oyako don in Japanese, where oyako refers to "parent and child", making reference to the use of chicken and eggs in the dish. This is popularly eaten for family lunches in Japan.

INGREDIENTS

Mirin	100 ml (3 1/3 fl oz)
Dark soy sauce	4 Tbsp
Boneless chicken thighs	400 g (14 1/3 oz), cut into bite-size pieces
White onions	2, medium, peeled
Eggs	6, lightly beaten and divided into 4 equal portions
Cooked Japanese short-grain rice	4 servings, kept warm
Trefoil (mitsuba)	1 small bunch, cut into 2.5-cm (1-in) lengths
Japanese seven-spice seasoning (shichimi togarashi) or ground Japanese pepper (sansho)	

DASHI

Water	200 ml (6 1/2 fl oz)
Dried kelp (konbu)	5-cm (2-in) piece
Bonito flakes	10 g (1/3 oz)

METHOD

- Prepare dashi. Refer to method on page 10.
- Put 150 ml (5 fl oz / ⅝ cup) dashi, mirin and soy sauce into a medium saucepan. Bring to the boil, then add chicken and onions. Reduce heat to medium and simmer for 3–5 minutes, covered. Remove from heat and divide into 4 equal portions.
- Prepare a single serve of chicken and eggs on rice. Pour 1 portion of chicken and onion mixture into an oyako pan. Bring to the boil and pour in three-quarters of a portion of eggs. Cover with a lid and simmer for about 30 seconds over medium-low heat, then remove lid and pour in remaining egg mixture. Cover and simmer for a few more seconds until mixture is almost set. Remove from heat.
- Gently slide chicken and egg mixture onto a serving bowl of rice. Garnish with trefoil and serve hot, sprinkled with seven-spice seasoning or Japanese pepper, if desired.
- Repeat cooking procedure with balance portions of chicken and onion mixture and eggs to prepare remaining 3 servings. Serve as you cook, as the dish should be eaten hot.

cold buckwheat noodles Serves 4

Soba noodles make a very healthy dish as they have a high content of vitamin B and protein. Substitute with dried or frozen wheat (udon) noodles for a variation to this recipe.

INGREDIENTS

Dried buckwheat noodles (soba)	400 g (14 1/3 oz)
Japanese spring onion (scallion)	1/4, finely sliced
Shredded dried seaweed (kizami nori)	4 Tbsp
Japanese seven-spice seasoning (shichimi togarashi)	to taste (optional)
Wasabi	to taste (optional)

DIPPING SAUCE

Dark soy sauce	3 Tbsp
Mirin	3 Tbsp

DASHI

Water	250 ml (8 fl oz / 1 cup)
Dried kelp (konbu)	5-cm (2-in) piece
Bonito flakes	10 g (1/3 oz)

METHOD

- Prepare dashi. Refer to method on page 10.
- Prepare dipping sauce. Combine 200 ml (6 1/2 fl oz) dashi, soy sauce and mirin in a small saucepan. Bring to the boil, then remove from heat immediately. Set aside to cool completely.
- Bring a large pot of water to the boil. Add noodles and cook for 5 minutes, or until just tender. (Refer to cooking instructions on packet of noodles, if unsure.) Drain noodles in a colander. Rinse and rub drained noodles for 1–2 minutes under cold running water. Drain well.
- Divide noodles among 4 individual serving plates. Sprinkle each plate with 1 Tbsp seaweed, spring onion and seven-spice seasoning, if desired. Divide dipping sauce among 4 bowls.
- Serve noodles with dipping sauce on the side, adding a dollop of wasabi to sauce, if desired.

mixed rice Serves 4

A wide variety of mixed rice dishes are available in Japanese cuisine. This particular dish is commonly packed into lunch boxes or served for simple home meals.

INGREDIENTS

Chicken thighs	150 g (5 1/3 oz), boned and cubed
Japanese short-grain rice	320 g (11 1/2 oz)
Short-grain glutinous rice	160 g (5 1/2 oz)
Sake	3 Tbsp
Dark soy sauce	2 Tbsp
Salt	1/2 tsp
Carrot	1, peeled and julienned
Honshimeji mushrooms	130 g (4 1/2 oz), ends trimmed
Deep-fried bean curd (abura age)	1, blanched, halved lengthways and cut crossways into long strips

CHICKEN MARINADE

Sake	1/2 Tbsp
Dark soy sauce	1 tsp

DASHI

Water	500 ml (16 fl oz / 2 cups)
Dried kelp (konbu)	6-cm (2 1/2-in) piece
Bonito flakes	15 g (1/2 oz)

METHOD

- Prepare dashi. Refer to method on page 10.
- Combine chicken cubes with ingredients for marinade. Set aside.
- Put both types of rice into a mixing bowl and fill with cold water. Stir quickly with fingers and drain. Press rice down repeatedly using your palm for 20–30 times to rub rice grains against one other. Refill bowl with tap water, then repeat process of rubbing and rinsing another 2–3 times until water almost runs clear. Soak washed rice in water for 30 minutes. Drain well and transfer to a rice cooker. Add 450 ml (14½ fl oz) dashi, sake, soy sauce and salt. Mix well.
- Layer chicken, carrot, mushrooms and bean curd on top of rice. Turn on rice cooker to cook rice. When rice is cooked, fold mixture gently with a wet Japanese spatula (shamoji). Mix well.
- Dish out to individual serving bowls. Garnish as desired and serve hot.

sukiyaki beef bowl Serves 4

Sukiyaki is a popular seasoning that usually comprises soy sauce, dashi, sake, sugar and mirin. Use beef belly for this dish, so its fat will melt while cooking and impart a wonderful flavour to the rice.

INGREDIENTS

Thinly sliced beef belly	400 g (14 1/3 oz)
Cooking oil	2 tsp
Dark soy sauce	4 Tbsp
Sugar	3 Tbsp
Sake	4 Tbsp
Mirin	2 Tbsp
White onion	1, large, peeled and cut into 12 wedges along the grain
Cooked Japanese short-grain rice	4 servings, kept warm
Egg yolks	4
Pickled red ginger	4 tsp
Chopped spring onion (scallion), green portion only	4 tsp
Japanese seven-spice seasoning (shichimi togarashi) (optional)	

DASHI

Water	200 ml (6 1/2 fl oz)
Dried kelp (konbu)	5-cm (2-in) piece
Bonito flakes	10 g (1/3 oz)

METHOD

- Prepare dashi. Refer to method on page 10.
- Cut beef belly crossways into 5-cm (2-in) wide pieces. Heat oil in a frying pan and stir-fry beef for 1 minute.
- Combine soy sauce and sugar in a small bowl until sugar is dissolved. Add mixture to pan and mix well. Cook for 1–2 minutes, then transfer to a plate and set aside.
- Using the same pan, add 150 ml (5 fl oz) dashi, sake and mirin. Heat and bring to the boil. Add onion and cook for 3–5 minutes until onion is soft.
- Return beef to pan and heat through for 1–2 minutes. Remove from heat.
- Divide beef and onion mixture equally among 4 serving bowls of rice.
- Top centre of each bowl with an egg yolk. Garnish each bowl with 1 tsp pickled red ginger and 1 tsp chopped spring onions. Sprinkle with Japanese seven-spice seasoning, if desired. Serve immediately.

red rice Serves 4

This is a traditional Japanese festive dish. It is often prepared and presented as a gift to relatives, neighbours and friends during special occasions such as birthdays and weddings.

INGREDIENTS

Japanese short-grain glutinous rice	480 g (17 oz)
Dried Japanese red beans (sasage or azuki)	60 g (2 oz), washed and drained
Water	600 ml (20 fl oz)
Toasted black sesame seeds	1 Tbsp
Salt	1/2 tsp

METHOD

- Prepare rice for cooking. Put rice into a mixing bowl and fill with cold tap water. Stir quickly with fingers and drain. Press rice down repeatedly using your palm for 20–30 times to rub rice grains against one another. Refill bowl with tap water, then repeat process of rubbing and rinsing another 2–3 times until water almost runs clear. Soak washed rice in water for 30–60 minutes. Drain well.
- Place red beans in a pot and cover with water. Bring to the boil for 1–2 minutes, then drain well. Return drained beans to pot and add 600 ml (20 fl oz) water. Heat and simmer for about 30 minutes, or until beans are soft. Strain to separate red beans and cooking liquid. Measure out 330 ml (11 fl oz) liquid for cooking rice. Discard any excess liquid, or top up with water, if amount is insufficient.
- Transfer drained rice, red beans and cooking liquid to a rice cooker and cook. When rice is cooked, fold mixture gently with a wet Japanese spatula (shamoji). Mix well.
- Transfer to serving bowls or a traditional Japanese lacquer box. Sprinkle black sesame seeds and salt over before serving.

rice balls with red bean paste Makes 20

Known as ohagi, the Japanese present these rice balls as a sweet offering to their ancestors during the week of the equinox.

INGREDIENTS

Glutinous rice	320 g (11 1/3 oz)
Castor (superfine) sugar	1/2 tsp

SOY BEAN POWDER COATING

Soy bean powder (kinako)	5 Tbsp
Castor (superfine) sugar	1 Tbsp

RED BEAN PASTE (ANKO)

Japanese red beans (adzuki)	500 g (1 lb 1 1/2 oz), washed and drained
Japanese sugar (jo haku to) or castor (superfine) sugar	430 g(15 1/3 oz)
Salt	1/2 tsp

METHOD

- Prepare red bean paste. Put red beans into a large pot and cover with water. Bring to the boil briefly, then remove from heat and drain. Return drained red beans to pot and add fresh water to fill up three-quarters of pot. Return to the boil, then reduce heat to low and simmer for 2 hours, or until beans are soft, skimming off any foam that rises to the surface. Remove from heat. Drain well. Return softened red beans to pot and add sugar. Cook over low heat, stirring constantly for 10 minutes until paste thickens. Add salt and stir to mix well. Remove from heat.

- Spread red bean paste out on a baking tray. Set aside to cool. Divide cooled red bean paste into 20 equal portions. Form into balls and arrange on a baking tray. Cover with plastic wrap and set aside.

- Refer to method on page 71 to prepare rice for cooking. Transfer rice to a rice cooker and top up with 400 ml (13 fl oz) water. Leave to soak for 30–60 minutes, then stir in sugar and turn on rice cooker. When rice is cooked, fold gently with a wet Japanese spatula (shamoji). Mix well. Using wet hands, divide rice into 20 equal portions and shape into balls. Place on a baking tray and set aside.
- Prepare red bean paste-coated rice balls. Place a ball of red bean paste on a small sheet of plastic, then flatten into a 10-cm (4-in) round. Top with a rice ball and gently mould red bean paste around it to enclose. Shape to form a smooth ball, then remove plastic and set aside. Repeat to make 9 more.
- Prepare soy bean powder-coated rice balls. Place a rice ball on a small sheet of plastic, then flatten into a 10-cm (4-in) round. Top with a ball of red bean paste and gently mould rice around it to enclose. Shape to form a smooth ball, then unwrap and set aside. Repeat to make 9 more. Coat each rice ball with soy bean powder, shaking off any excess.
- Transfer both types of rice balls onto a serving plate. Serve immediately.

candied sweet potatoes Serves 4

This dessert is known as daigaku imo in Japanese. Daigaku means "university", and the origins of this dish can be traced back to a shop which was located in front of Tokyo University nearly a century ago.

INGREDIENTS

Japanese sweet potatoes	400 g (14 1/3 oz), scrubbed and rinsed with skin
Cooking oil for deep-frying	
Sugar	5 Tbsp
Water	2 Tbsp
Dark soy sauce	1 tsp
Toasted black sesame seeds	1 tsp

METHOD

- Cut sweet potatoes lengthways into 1.5 x 1.5 x 6-cm (3/4 x 3/4 x 2 1/2-in) strips. Soak in water for 10–15 minutes. Drain.
- Cook sweet potatoes in the microwave oven on high, or steam over high heat for 5 minutes. Remove and pat dry. Set aside.
- Heat oil to 160°–170°C (325°–340°F). Deep-fry sweet potatoes for 2–3 minutes, or until light brown. Remove and drain thoroughly on kitchen paper. Set aside.
- Combine sugar, water and soy sauce in a non-stick frying pan over medium heat. Stir continuously until sugar has dissolved completely. Continue to cook for another 2–3 minutes until bubbles appear on the surface, and sauce has thickened and turned glossy. Remove from heat.
- Coat sweet potatoes evenly with sauce. Transfer to a serving plate and sprinkle with black sesame seeds. Serve immediately.

rice ball skewers Makes about 30 rice balls

You can find this popular dessert at any traditional confectionery shop in Japan. It remains a perennial favourite of both the young and old.

INGREDIENTS

Japanese rice flour (jo shin ko)	250 g (9 oz)
Sugar	1 Tbsp
Warm water	220 ml (7 1/3 fl oz)
Bamboo skewers	10, soaked in water for 5 minutes, then drained

SWEET SOY SAUCE (MITARASHI ANN)

Water	100 ml (3 1/3 fl oz)
Dark soy sauce	70 ml (2 1/3 fl oz)
Mirin	1 Tbsp
Sugar	90 g (3 oz)
Potato flour (potato starch)	15 g (1/2 oz), mixed with 1 Tbsp water

METHOD

- Prepare rice balls. Combine rice flour and sugar in a mixing bowl. Add warm water and stir to mix well. Knead to form a medium-soft dough. Divide dough into 5–6 equal portions. Form into balls, then flatten into circles.
- Line the bottom of a preheated steamer with a piece of wet muslin cloth. Place dough circles into steamer. Cover and steam over high heat for about 15 minutes or until cooked.
- Remove and transfer steamed dough circles into a wet grinding bowl (suribachi). Using a wet pestle, pound and mash dough circles together to obtain an elastic and soft dough. Divide and shape cooked dough into balls, each weighing about 15 g (1/2 oz). This recipe should yield about 30 rice balls.

- Skewer 3 rice balls onto each bamboo stick. Repeat until ingredients are used up. Preheat a metal grill over a gas hob until red-hot. Grill each stick of rice balls for 3 seconds on each side or until rice balls are seared with brown grill marks. Repeat until all rice balls are grilled. Set aside.
- Prepare sweet soy sauce. Combine water, soy sauce, mirin and sugar in a small saucepan. Heat and bring to the boil. Stir in potato flour mixture and cook until sauce has thickened and turned glossy. Remove from heat.
- Dip each stick of rice balls into sweet soy sauce to coat evenly. Serve warm.

pancakes with red bean paste Makes 8

Traditionally made up of red bean paste sandwiched between two pancakes, this snack, known as dora yaki in Japanese, takes its name from the dora, a little percussion instrument that the snack resembles.

INGREDIENTS

Plain (all-purpose) flour	100 g (3½ oz)
Baking powder	½ tsp
Eggs	2
Castor (superfine) sugar	90 g (3 oz)
Honey	1 Tbsp
Mirin	1 Tbsp
Water	2 Tbsp
Cooking oil for pan-frying	
Candied chestnuts	8, cut into small pieces

RED BEAN PASTE (ANKO)

Japanese red beans (azuki)	500 g (1 lb 1½ oz), washed and drained
Japanese sugar (jo haku to) or castor (superfine) sugar	430 g (15⅓ oz)
Salt	½ tsp

METHOD

- Refer to method on page 72 for preparing red bean paste. Weigh cooled red bean paste to obtain 240 g (8 1/2 oz) as filling for pancakes. Divide into equal portions of 30 g (1 oz) each and arrange on a baking tray. Cover with plastic wrap and set aside.
- Sift flour and baking powder together twice. Set aside. Beat eggs and sugar in another bowl until mixture is very pale and thick. Add honey, mirin and water. Combine well to obtain a smooth mixture. Using a rubber spatula spoon, gradually fold flour into egg mixture to obtain a smooth batter. Cover with plastic wrap and set aside at room temperature for about 20 minutes.
- Heat a little oil in a non–stick frying pan over low heat. Remove from heat and rest bottom of pan on a piece of damp cloth. Pour in about 3 Tbsp batter, then swirl pan to obtain an 8-cm (3-in) circle. Return pan to heat and cook over low heat for 1 minute until bubbles appear on surface of pancake and underside is brown. Turn pancake over and pan-fry other side for a few seconds until brown. Remove cooked pancake and repeat to make more pancakes until batter is used up. There should be about 16 pancakes in total.
- Top half the pancakes, each, with a portion of red bean paste and some candied chestnut pieces. Sandwich with remaining pancakes. Serve warm or at room temperature.

weights and measures

Quantities for this book are given in Metric, Imperial and American (spoon and cup) measures. Standard spoon and cup measurements used are: 1 tsp = 5 ml, 1 Tbsp = 15 ml, 1 cup = 250 ml. All measures are level unless otherwise stated.

Liquid And Volume Measures

Metric	*Imperial*	*American*
5 ml	1/6 fl oz	1 teaspoon
10 ml	1/3 fl oz	1 dessertspoon
15 ml	1/2 fl oz	1 tablespoon
60 ml	2 fl oz	1/4 cup (4 tablespoons)
85 ml	2 1/2 fl oz	1/3 cup
90 ml	3 fl oz	3/8 cup (6 tablespoons)
125 ml	4 fl oz	1/2 cup
180 ml	6 fl oz	3/4 cup
250 ml	8 fl oz	1 cup
300 ml	10 fl oz (1/2 pint)	1 1/4 cups
375 ml	12 fl oz	1 1/2 cups
435 ml	14 fl oz	1 3/4 cups
500 ml	16 fl oz	2 cups
625 ml	20 fl oz (1 pint)	2 1/2 cups
750 ml	24 fl oz (1 1/5 pints)	3 cups
1 litre	32 fl oz (1 3/5 pints)	4 cups
1.25 litres	40 fl oz (2 pints)	5 cups
1.5 litres	48 fl oz (2 2/5 pints)	6 cups
2.5 litres	80 fl oz (4 pints)	10 cups

Oven Temperature

	°C	*°F*	*Gas Regulo*
Very slow	120	250	1
Slow	150	300	2
Moderately slow	160	325	3
Moderate	180	350	4
Moderately hot	190/200	375/400	5/6
Hot	210/220	410/425	6/7
Very hot	230	450	8
Super hot	250/290	475/550	9/10

Dry Measures

Metric	*Imperial*
30 grams	1 ounce
45 grams	1 1/2 ounces
55 grams	2 ounces
70 grams	2 1/2 ounces
85 grams	3 ounces
100 grams	3 1/2 ounces
110 grams	4 ounces
125 grams	4 1/2 ounces
140 grams	5 ounces
280 grams	10 ounces
450 grams	16 ounces (1 pound)
500 grams	1 pound, 1 1/2 ounces
700 grams	1 1/2 pounds
800 grams	1 3/4 pounds
1 kilogram	2 pounds, 3 ounces
1.5 kilograms	3 pounds, 4 1/2 ounces
2 kilograms	4 pounds, 6 ounces

Length

Metric	*Imperial*
0.5 cm	1/4 inch
1 cm	1/2 inch
1.5 cm	3/4 inch
2.5 cm	1 inch

Abbreviation

tsp	teaspoon
Tbsp	tablespoon
g	gram
kg	kilogram
ml	millilitre